SUPERNATURAL WEIGHT LOSS

IN THE

C⚖URTS

OF

HEAVEN

PRAYERS AND DECLARATIONS THAT BREAK
THE POWER OF CRAVINGS, FOOD ADDICTION
& THE ENDLESS CYCLE OF YO-YO DIETING

SUPERNATURAL WEIGHT LOSS

IN THE — COURTS — OF — HEAVEN

PRAYERS AND DECLARATIONS THAT BREAK
THE POWER OF CRAVINGS, FOOD ADDICTION
& THE ENDLESS CYCLE OF YO-YO DIETING

BRUCE W. TOWNSEND

DEDICATION

This book is dedicated to Bishop Bill Hamon of Christian International and the father of the modern-day prophetic movement. Thank you for your encouragement, prophetic words, instruction, and fatherly advice to make me also a reproducer who reproduces reproducers.

THANK YOU

Thank you for choosing to read *Supernatural Weight Loss in the Courts of Heaven*. I pray this book will bless you to transform your mind and body.

As a thank you, I want to give you the audio version of this book to help you learn and apply the keys inside this book at an accelerated rate by listening and reading.

To download your free copy of the audiobook version, please visit:

Gift.CourtsofHeavenWeightLoss.com

Thank you for buying my book.

TABLE OF CONTENTS

FOREWORD

B ruce Townsend presents faith-based principles that will build your confidence that you can lose weight and break addictions to live a healthy long life.

These principles will work for all who practice them, but they work best for those who know God and how to present your need to Him with faith that God will help all that call upon Him.

Those Christians who know the scripture that declares our bodies have become a habitation of God like the temple was for the Israelites would not knowingly destroy the temple in any way, yet many Christians are destroying God's temple, which their body is with all the wrong ways presented in this book.

The author emphasizes that God's medicine chest is composed of natural healing and the power of God's word for the Holy Spirit's supernatural healing.

This could be the book that reveals to you other areas than just eating that affect your body to lose weight. The mindsets and soul wounds that one has can hinder or help overcome all hindrances. This book will help renew your way of thinking and talking so that habit patterns are removed that hinder your successful living in body, soul, and spirit.

You will discover that the faith decrees you make are the supernatural weapons God has given you to execute the right verdicts in the Word of God which have been issued from the courts of heaven.

As Christians, we must realize our battle is not just with appetite, weight, and wrong habit patterns but against demonic spirits which Satan assigns against us to keep us in bondage.

But you will understand and know the truth that will make you completely free to live a healthy life with proper habits and free from all demonic influences in your life. When you change your attitude, words, and thoughts you change your body and habit pattern to successful living.

Why not put this book to the test and you may discover the answers to your desires and receive the results you have been looking for?

Bishop Bill Hamon
Christian International Apostolic-Global Network

INTRODUCTION

It is not necessarily your fault

You may think that you have tried everything to lose weight: diets, counting calories, keto, paleo, exercise, gastric band surgery, diet foods, pills, and potions, yet nothing worked.

The weight loss industry is a failed system marketing almost instant hope with methods and products that are not working for the majority. The statistics below show evidence for this, revealing that half of the United Stat population attempts to lose weight while still, 73% are overweight or obese.

That number has increasingly become a failure. It is an $80 billion industry, and Americans are fatter than ever. Money spent is not translating into thinner hips or waistlines.

America is experiencing the worst pandemic in history that statistically kills more Christians than non-believers. The pandemic is obesity, a demonic strategy to hinder the Gospel of Jesus Christ and rob the believer of living a victorious life of blessing and health. This pandemic is impacting the advancement of the Kingdom of God as God's children are getting sick and dying prematurely.

Facts and statistics

1. Over 73% of U.S. Adults Overweight or Obese.

   "Obesity rate up by half since 1999-2000. In national data from the survey period of 1960-1962, only about 13.4% of adults had obesity and less than 1% had severe obesity. And during that same survey period, about 31.5% of American adults were considered overweight."[1]

2. Obesity affects 1 in 5 children in the United States.

   "For children and adolescents aged 2-19 years in 2017-2021, the prevalence of obesity was 19.7% and affected about 14.7 million children and adolescents." [2]

3. Over 60 chronic diseases are linked to obesity.

   "If you are overweight or have obesity, your risk for dozens of diseases and conditions is higher. These include type 2 diabetes, heart disease, stroke, cancer, and many other diseases." [3]

4. Obesity is costly.

   "According to estimates, the national cost of obesity is $122 billion per year – mostly in healthcare costs."

   "Per year, the cost of obesity for a man is $2,646. Adding in the value of lost life, the cost increases to $6,518. For a woman, the individual cost of obesity annually amounts to

---

[1] Kristen Monaco, "*Over 73% of U.S. Adults Overweight or Obese*," *MedPage Today*, 11 December 2020, medpagetoday.com/primarycare/obesity/90142.
[2] "*Childhood Obesity Facts*," Centers for Disease Control and Prevention, cdc.gov/obesity/data/childhood.html
[3] Kimberley Holland, "*Obesity Facts*, Healthline*," 18 January 2022, healthline.com/health/obesity-facts

$4,879. Again, adding in the value of lost life, a woman's individual expense of obesity comes to $8,365." [4]

5. Americans' calorie consumption is at an all-time high.

"The average American consumes more than 3,600 calories daily – a 24% increase from 1961, when the average was just 2,880 calories. Americans have not increased their consumption of all food and drink evenly, however — our alcohol intake peaked in the 1980s, but our growing consumption of vegetable oils alone accounts for more than half of the calorie spike." [5]

6. Excess weight will shorten a lifespan.

"The results showed that participants with BMI of 22.5-<25 kg/m2 (considered a healthy weight range) had the lowest mortality risk during the time they were followed. The risk of mortality increased significantly throughout the overweight range: a BMI of 25-<27.5 kg/m2 was associated with a 7% higher risk of mortality; a BMI of 27.5-<30 kg/m2 was associated with a 20% higher risk; a BMI of 30.0-<35.0 kg/m2 was associated with a 45% higher risk; a BMI of 35.0-<40.0 kg/m2 was associated with a 94% higher risk; and a BMI of 40.0-<60.0 kg/m2 was associated with a nearly three-fold risk. Every 5 units higher BMI above 25 kg/m2 was associated with about 31% higher risk of

[4] Lyle Johnson, "The Hidden Cost of Obesity: It's More Expensive than You May Think," Houston Surgical Specialists, 27 June 2022, doctormarvin.com/cost-of-obesity/hidden-cost-obesity-expensive-may-think/

[5] Emma Fierberg and Skye Gould, "Here's how the American diet has changed in the last 52 years," Business Insider, 13 June 2017, businessinsider.com/american-calorie-intake-last-52-years-diet-food-eating-increase-science-2017-6#

premature death. Participants who were underweight also had a higher mortality risk."

"Looking at specific causes of death, the study found that, **for each 5-unit increase in BMI above 25 kg/ m2, the corresponding increases in risk were 49% for cardiovascular mortality, 38% for respiratory disease mortality, and 19% for cancer mortality.**" [6]

"Obesity has a similar impact on life expectancy. But while smoking certainly carries numerous and substantial health risks, obesity poses even more."

"A 2019 study of nearly 450,000 people in PLoS Genetics linked excessive weight to coronary artery disease, stroke, type 1 and 2 diabetes, chronic obstructive pulmonary disease (COPD), chronic liver disease, renal failure, and lung cancer."

"According to a Lancet review of 57 studies, obese people ages 40 to 45 can expect an eight to 10 year loss of life expectancy." [7]

7. Christians are 50% more likely to become obese than non-Christians.

"A surprising new link between obesity and regular religious participation has been discovered amongst God-fearing believers."

---

[6] Todd Datz and Dr. Emanuele Di Angelantonio, "As overweight and obesity increase, so does risk of dying prematurely," Harvard T. H. Chan School of Public Health, July 2016, www.hsph.harvard.edu/news/press-releases/overweight-obesity-mortality-risk/

[7] Mark Stibich, PhD., "Is Smoking Worse Than Being Obese?" Very Well health, Updated April 26, 2020, https://www.verywellhealth.com/which-is-worse-smoking-or-being-obese-2224333

"The study conducted by author Matthew J. Feinstein found that young adults who regularly attended religious services were fifty percent more likely to become obese by the time they reached middle age." [8]

8. "Nearly one-half (49.1%) of adults tried to lose weight within the last 12 months." [9]

Weight gain can rob you of your destiny

You could die at least eight years too early and lose all impact you could have had upon advancing the Kingdom of God on the earth, cutting your destiny short if you are a slave to your appetite, ruled over by a fork.

You may be ignorant of the other factors causing obesity, such as environment, soul wounds, and franken-foods (fabricated substances masquerading as food). Darkness or ignorance is where Satan rules, as he is the prince or ruler of darkness.

He masters the ignorant. Your defense is to arm yourself with knowledge of the Word and understand the relationship between food and physical dysfunctions.

Amazingly, American churches are silent on this pandemic and do not oppose Satan's rule of darkness over this tragedy. Because of silence and ignorance, the Kingdom of Darkness can gain access to your life. He searches for unguarded hearts.

---

[8] Eryn Sun, "Firm Faith, Fat Body? Study Finds High Rate of Obesity among Religious," *Christian Post*, March 24, 2027, www.christianpost.com/news/firm-faith-fat-body-study-finds-high-rate-of-obesity-among-religious.html
[9] Crestin B. Martin, "Attempts to Lose Weight Among Adults in the United States," *2013–2016*, July 2018, https://www.cdc.gov/nchs/products/databriefs/db313.htm

Watch over your heart with all diligence, For from it flow the springs of life.

–*Proverbs 4:23 (NASB)*

If you do not submit yourself to God concerning your body and health—and fail to resist Satan's rule over your body—you invite him to enter, kill, steal, and destroy by default.

Satan's strategy is to attempt to kill you early and to hinder the Gospel by making you weak and sick without effective opposition. Weakness and sickness will hinder you in fulfilling your divine assignment to share the Gospel of the Kingdom.

If you do not begin to control your weight, you will invite chronic diseases to enter your life.

Lose weight by grace vs. lose weight by works and self-discipline

For by grace you have been saved through faith; and this is not of yourselves, it is the gift of God; not a result of works, so that no one may boast. For we are His workmanship, created in Christ Jesus for good works, which God prepared beforehand so that we would walk in them.

–*Ephesians 2:8-10*

It is a rare person who seeks the Lord for wisdom and plans to lose weight. Most people use self-discipline from a works mentality. They believe they can save or deliver themselves without Christ. The works mentality is functional atheism.

In the thirty-ninth year of his reign Asa became diseased in his feet. His disease was severe, yet even in his disease he did not seek the Lord, but the physicians. So Asa lay down with his fathers and died in the forty-first year of his reign.

–2 Chronicles 16:12-13

Asa stopped seeking the Lord as he used to do in former times to follow the world's systems for his health. Egyptians trained these physicians in their idolatrous form of medicine. The result is that Asa died.

Learn from Asa's example of failure to always be mindful of seeking the Lord first in everything, including your health and weight.

All self-deliverance is idolatrous. The opposite of this is that Christ empowers us to do all things.

I can do all things through Him who strengthens me.

–Philippians 4:13

Self-sufficiency, self-works, and pride are strongholds of darkness. Humility is the stronghold of the righteous.

It is impossible to please God without faith. If you are not using your faith to overcome the weight gain battle, you do not please God in this area and are also damaging the temple of the Holy Spirit.

And without faith it is impossible to please Him, for the one who comes to God must believe that He exists, and that He proves to be One who rewards those who seek Him.

–Hebrews 11:6

This book aims to help you build your faith so you can lose weight God's way and glorify Him in your body, which belongs to Him.

Summary of keys to Supernatural Weight Loss in the Courts of Heaven

Key 1 – *Discern the Spiritual War on Your Weight.* This key will unlock revelation that will help you to discern demonic spiritual war raging against your soul to wound you and rob your life and health.

Key 2 – *Renew Your Mind.* Why willpower will not help you permanently lose weight and how to stop the warfare raging against your soul that causes you to gain weight.

Key 3 – *Prosecute Food Addictions and Altars in the Courts of Heaven.* This key reveals how to break Satan's legal rights to keep you sick and overweight.

Key 4 – *File a Lawsuit in the Courts of Heaven to Lose Weight.* This key reveals how to file a lawsuit against evil altars and idols and obtain a legal verdict in your favor for freedom from sickness and excess weight.

Key 5 – *Pray & Make Faith Decrees.* This key reveals scriptures, prayers, and faith decrees to enforce the judicial verdict and allow you to lose weight without struggle.

KEY I

DISCERN THE SPIRITUAL
WAR ON YOUR WEIGHT

Deliverance from Satan's fat trap

Here are the leading physical causes of obesity

- Poor diet
- Calories
- Lack of exercise
- Medical reasons such as hormonal imbalance
- Toxins
- Genetics

The actual root cause for these physical causes is Satan's strategy to make you sick and kill you prematurely, thereby removing you from the earth that he wants to control.

Obesity is very high and continues to increase, despite all the products and services promoted to lose weight. Most people neglect the root problem, which is a spiritual stronghold.

"Worldwide obesity has nearly tripled since 1975." [10]

Obesity has tripled in a mere 47 years, even though there are gyms, personal trainers, weight loss products, YouTube videos, online courses, diet drinks, and foods everywhere you turn.

The war on obesity is a war that Americans are overwhelmingly losing. Just knowing these natural causes and trying to fix them is not

---

[10] World Health Organization, "Obesity and Overweight," June 9, 2021, www.who.int/news-room/fact-sheets/detail/obesity-and-overweight

working for the vast majority. The problem does not begin in the physical realm.

> *For though we walk in the flesh, we do not wage battle according to the flesh, for the weapons of our warfare are not of the flesh, but divinely powerful for the destruction of fortresses. We are destroying arguments and all arrogance raised against the knowledge of God, and we are taking every thought captive to the obedience of Christ, and we are ready to punish all disobedience, whenever your obedience is complete.*
>
> *–2 Corinthians 10:3-6*

It is not your body or your flesh that you need to battle. Satan is the enemy your focus should be on.

Are you wrestling with your own body when you try to lose weight, unaware that this is a spiritual war? Unless you use supernatural weapons, you are likely to fail in your efforts to lose weight, as most people do.

The fat is the result of Satan's trap, and to escape the web, you must submit wholeheartedly to the Lord and resist the devil so that he will flee.

> *Submit, therefore to God. But resist the devil, and he will flee from you.*
>
> *–James 4:7*

"...the foundation in our continued success in warfare comes from yielding to the Lord as He reveals these strongholds and agreeing with Him through repentance in pulling them down." [11]

The weight problem is not your fault. Because, fundamentally, it is a demonic strategy unleashed against you of which you were unaware.

He battles against your mind and emotions with ignorance, advertising for junk foods, stress, toxins in your food and environment, hormones in your food, and destructive relationships with food by using food for comfort and a stress reliever.

Unless you destroy these strongholds with supernatural weapons, you will remain a slave to your appetites or a slave to dysfunctions in your body, such as hormonal imbalances or gut imbalances, and all the natural weight loss solutions will not work for you.

"The devil can traffic in any area of darkness, even the darkness that exists in a Christian's heart." [12]

Darkness is synonymous with ignorance and light with knowledge. The weight problem is simply a result of a lack of knowledge of what the Bible says about the war you have had over your weight and health.

My people are destroyed for lack of knowledge. Since you have rejected knowledge, I also will reject you from being My priest. Since you have forgotten the Law of your God, I also will forget your children.

–Hosea 4:6

[11] Francis Frangipane, "The Three Battlegrounds," USA: Advancing Church Publications, 1989, p.22
[12] Francis Frangipane, "The Three Battlegrounds," USA: Advancing Church Publications, 1989, p. 4

Satan's strategic objective is to prevent you from fulfilling your assignment of the Great Commission to disciple the nations and advance the Kingdom of God.

Satan does not care if you go to Heaven. His only concern is that you are out of his way on earth. His goal is to defeat you on earth to stop believers from transferring the Kingdom of Heaven to earth by causing sickness and premature death. His strategy is to send you to Heaven early so you will not oppose his rule.

> *Your Kingdom come, Your will be done, On earth as it is in Heaven.*
>
> *—Matthew 6:10*

When your body is healthy, you will be at optimal weight

Excess weight is a sickness. You have a covenant right to seek healing according to scripture.

> "**Sickness**—Disease; malady; a morbid state of the body of an animal or plant, in which the organs do not perfectly perform their natural functions. Himself took our infirmities and bore our sicknesses. Matthew 8:17." [13]

Excess fat indicates that the body's organs are not performing their natural functions. Therefore, being overweight is a state of disease, and Christ redeemed you from the curse of sickness.

---

[13] Noah Webster, "American Dictionary of the English Language," Webster's Dictionary 1828, https://webstersdictionary1828.com/Dictionary/sickness

Christ redeemed us from the curse of the Law, having become a curse for us—for it is written: "Cursed is everyone who hangs on a tree"— in order that in Christ Jesus the blessing of Abraham would come to the Gentiles so that we would receive the promise of the Spirit through faith.

–Galatians 3:13-14

Do not allow Satan to deceive you into focusing on the extra weight and ignoring your state of health. Make it your goal to receive healing naturally and supernaturally. You will know you are healthy when the Lord transforms your body to your optimal weight.

Food cravings can also have a natural cause within your gut.

"If you find yourself craving sugar and processed carbs and starches, it is because of an overgrowth of bacteria inside your colon—in your gut. There are several key classes of bacteria that live inside your colon. Microbiome, the good flora in our gut that heals our immune system. Firmicutes are a family of bacteria in the gut that causes us to extract more calories out of the food and can make us fat. It changes our taste so that we crave more super sweetness. Bacteroidetes are a family of healthy bacteria that cause us to desire healthy foods." [14]

---

[14] Kenneth Copeland and Don and Mary Colbert, "The healthy Gut Zone,," The Believer's Voice of Victory Broadcast Notes, August 16-20, 2021, p. 4

Three medicines that create life from God's medicine chest

God did not create His medicine chest from chemicals from the dirt. His medicine chest is composed of plants for natural healing and the power of His Word and the Holy Spirit for supernatural healing. The Word of God proclaims plants for both food and medicine.

> Then God said, "Behold, I have given you every plant yielding seed that is on the surface of all the earth, and every tree which has fruit yielding seed; it shall be food for you;
>
> *–Genesis 1:29*
>
> in the middle of its street. On either side of the river was the tree of life, bearing twelve kinds of fruit, yielding its fruit every month; and the leaves of the tree were for the healing of the nations.
>
> *–Revelation 22:2*

Here are powerful life-giving examples of God's medicine chest:

Cayenne

Cayenne is a fantastic herb. Reports reveal that cayenne has stopped heart attacks or strokes within 30 seconds when it is hot enough, such as 150,000 heat units or more. There must be a sufficient dosage for this to work. Cayenne can stop bleeding by packing it into a wound or consuming it internally to stop hemorrhaging.

The amazing thing about this is that it will stop a bleeding nose from the result of an injury, but if the nose is bleeding because of a stroke, it will not stop it.

How does the cayenne know? God has designed intelligence in the plant that man can never create in a lab.

Gingko Bilboa

Approximately 170 ginkgo trees survived the Hiroshima atomic blast from WWII, and all the trees are still alive 77 years later. That is a large dose of life to survive an atomic bomb.

Olive tree

The average lifespan for an olive tree is five hundred years. When Jesus prayed in the Garden of Gethsemane, the olive trees were one thousand years old. Now over two thousand years later, those trees are still alive. Is it any wonder that God chose olive oil as the base for anointing the sick or anointing for service and ministry?

"Let food be thy medicine, and let medicine be thy food." [15]

Death by fork

The first temptation of mankind was related to food.

> *The Lord God commanded the man, saying, "From any tree of the garden you may freely eat; but from the tree of the knowledge of good and evil you shall not eat, for on the day that you eat from it you will certainly die.*
>
> –Genesis 2:16-17

What may you freely eat? You may eat everything growing in God's Garden. The Garden provided everything man needed and wanted

---

[15] Source unknown

nutritionally. Natural food that God created is in God's medicine cabinet.

Life is in the seed. God gave man the first gift after blessing him with the dominion mandate. That gift was every seed-bearing tree or herb.

> Then God said, "Let the earth sprout vegetation, plants yielding seed, and fruit trees on the earth bearing fruit according to their kind with seed in them"; and it was so. Then God said, "Behold, I have given you every plant yielding seed that is on the surface of all the earth, and every tree which has fruit yielding seed; it shall be food for you;
>
> –Genesis 1:11, 29

When you plant a seed that God created, it will grow by itself and produce food because there is inherently life in the seed.

Frankenfoods are the serpent's food

Plant a synthetic vitamin pill or medicine pill made from chemicals and petroleum in the ground; what do you think will grow there? Nothing because there is no life in those substances.

Fake foods, otherwise known as *Frankenfoods*, created by man from petroleum and other chemicals, or processed food with these chemicals, are foreign to our bodies. Therefore, they cause disease and death. God did not design your body to process chemicals; he designed it to process food.

If you struggle with a disease— and being overweight is a disease—and you swallow these chemical pills, how do you think you will get life from something dead? According to Genesis's seedtime and harvesttime principle, everything produces after its kind. The dead thing you eat reproduces disease and death in you, not life.

Life creates life, so food and medicine must come from life to create health.

The chemicals you may be eating are the serpent's food. When you eat the serpent's food, you empower Satan to afflict you with disease and premature death because this is his food, not the food God gave you.

Demons do not have bodies. They can only express themselves through people or animals. Food addictions are the result of demonic spirits lusting to eat, but they have to use your body to manifest their nature.

They are spirits, so they cannot eat anything physical, including dirt. The way they express their nature then is to influence you to eat food or swallow pills that come from dirt or real food contaminated with these chemicals from the dirt.

> *Then the Lord God said to the serpent,*
> *"Because you have done this,*
> *Cursed are you more than all the livestock,*
> *And more than any animal of the field;*
> *On your belly you shall go,*
> *And dust you shall eat*
> *All the days of your life.*
>
> *—Genesis 3:14*

Let them eat plastic

Fake or modified foods created in a lab sow death in the body and create obesity.

If stubborn fat refuses to leave no matter what you do, it is probably a result of toxins, such as pesticides and herbicides, as well as plastic toxins that are abundant in our food, drinks, and even the air we breathe. Plastic toxins and chemical obesogens are major sources of obesity.

> "Changes in diet and exercise do not fully explain the steep rise in overweight and obesity over recent decades. One theory claims that chemicals in everyday plastic products promote weight gain by changing human metabolism."

> "A new study found that a range of plastic household items contain thousands of chemicals, many of them unknown. One-third of the items contained chemicals that, after extraction, caused the growth and proliferation of mouse fat cells in the lab." [16]

Plastic toxicity solutions

Try to reduce foods and beverages from plastic packaging and containers.

Eat cruciferous vegetables because they help detox plastic from the body.

Use a high-quality vacuum and get a high-quality air purifier to eliminate plastic toxins in the air within your home. Indoor pollution is much higher than outdoor pollution.

---

[16] James Kingsland, "Chemicals in everyday plastic items may lead to weight gain," Medical News Today, February 1, 2022, https://www.medicalnewstoday.com/articles/chemicals-in-everyday-plastic-items-may-lead-to-weight-gain

Are you digging a grave with your spoon?

The Israelites rebelled against God because of food idols in the wilderness. Because of their sin of food idolatry, a curse of a plague came upon them.

> *Now the rabble who were among them had greedy cravings; and the sons of Israel also wept again and said, "Who will give us meat to eat? We remember the fish which we used to eat for free in Egypt, the cucumbers, the melons, the leeks, the onions, and the garlic; but now our appetite is gone. There is nothing at all to look at except this manna!*
>
> *—Numbers 11:4-6*

> *Now a wind burst forth from the Lord and it brought quail from the sea, and dropped them beside the camp, about a day's journey on this side and a day's journey on the other side all around the camp, and about two cubits deep on the surface of the ground. And the people spent all that day, all night, and all the next day, and they gathered the quail (the one who gathered least gathered ten homers) and spread them out for themselves all around the camp. While the meat was still between their teeth, before it was chewed, the anger of the Lord was kindled against the people, and the Lord struck the people with a very severe plague. So that place was named Kibroth-hattaavah, because there they buried the people who had been greedy. From Kibroth-hattaavah the people set out for Hazeroth, and they remained at Hazeroth.*
>
> *—Numbers 11:31-35*

Kibroth-hattaavah means the graves of greed, lust, or covetousness.

God is warning you, just as He did the Israelites, that if you pursue food idols, you will fall into a grave of lust. However, Jesus is our faithful advocate in the Courts of Heaven to deliver us from idols and the curse so we will not be buried in these graves.

Most chronic diseases will have their roots in food idolatry or stress, and stress can relate to idolatry also.

Jesus also faced a temptation over food and idols during His 40-day fast in the wilderness.

> *Then Jesus was led up by the Spirit into the wilderness to be tempted by the devil. And after He had fasted for forty days and forty nights, He then became hungry. And the tempter came and said to Him, "If You are the Son of God, command that these stones become bread." But He answered and said, "It is written: 'Man shall not live on bread alone, but on every word that comes out of the mouth of God.'*
>
> *–Matthew 4:1-4*

Jesus defeated the devil's trap by speaking the Word to destroy temptation. By His example, Jesus showed us the way out of every temptation and how to defeat every problem, including the overweight problem.

> *And do not lead us into temptation, but deliver us from evil.*
>
> *–Matthew 6:13*

We should therefore pray that our Heavenly Father does not lead us into the temptation of food addictions, unhealthy lifestyles, and toxic thinking and emotions but delivers us from the evil one's lures and traps.

The Deliverance from Excess Weight Prayer

I assume that as a Christian that you are going to pray and ask the Lord to bless your food and thank Him for it before you eat. Why not modify your prayer by using the one in Chapter 5 under the subheading, *Prayer before meals and snacks*?

What do you think will happen if you pray that way before every meal? I can tell you exactly what will happen. Your faith will rise to a new height. You will be free of food idols, and you will lose weight.

The Spirit of God will lead you instead of your stomach or taste buds leading you.

You cannot pray and speak the Word continually and remain Satan's prisoner simultaneously. You will walk free every time according to your faith.

You do not have a weight problem; you have an idolatry problem. All you need is faith in God and His Word.

> *But Jesus said to him, "'If You can?' All things are possible for the one who believes.*
>
> *–Mark 9:23*

Soul wounds

Chronic weight issues are typically the result of soul wounds, such as trauma, injustice, betrayal, shame, abandonment, poverty, chronic sickness, discouragement, or emotional torture. Sins also relate to soul wounds because unrepented sins scar the soul and harden the heart.

You must remove arrow tips from your soul to not only receive inner healing, but frequently, it is the underlying cause of physical disease and dysfunctions, including weight gain.

> *Therefore, since we also have such a great cloud of witnesses surrounding us, let's rid ourselves of every obstacle and the sin which so easily entangles us, and let's run with endurance the race that is set before us, looking only at Jesus, the originator and perfecter of the faith, who for the joy set before Him endured the cross, despising the shame, and has sat down at the right hand of the throne of God.*
>
> *–Hebrews 12:1-2*

The word "obstacle" above can also be translated from Greek as *wound* or *arrow tip*. The idea here is that the arrow tip of a soul wound has penetrated the Christian. The wound weighs you down and thereby slows you down as you try to run the course of destiny that the Lord has chosen for you.

The revelation knowledge you receive from this book is designed to reveal that arrow tips remain in you. Use the tools here to remove the arrow tip, heal the soul wounds, and transform your mind and body so you can accelerate your progress on the divine path of destiny.

Scripture directs us to use our shield of faith to quench every flaming arrow the enemy shoots at us. If we fail to use the shield of faith, Satan will afflict us with soul wounds, or arrow tips, piercing our inner man.

> *in addition to all, taking up the shield of faith with which you will be able to extinguish all the flaming arrows of the evil one.*
>
> *–Ephesians 6:16*

A healed soul is a prosperous soul, and a prosperous soul produces a healthy body that remains at a healthy weight. If you have a wounded soul instead of a prosperous soul, Satan will find common ground within you that he may legally use to bring curses upon your life, including sickness and weight gain.

> *Beloved, I pray that in all respects you may prosper and be in good health, just as your soul prospers.*
>
> *−3 John 2*

Most, if not all, weight issues are going to be a result of this type of warfare. The rest of this book will focus on how to help you win this battle and break Satan's legal right to hinder and vex you so that you may receive the blessing of divine health in your body and optimize your weight.

Action Steps

1. Write down everything you can think of that hinders you from losing weight, whether food cravings, no time to exercise, eating from fast-food restaurants for convenience, or any other hindrance.

2. Choose just one of the problems you listed and ask the Lord to give you wisdom for a strategy to solve that problem.

3. Pray the *Deliverance from Excess Weight Prayer* before every meal and every snack.

KEY 2

RENEW THE MIND

Repentance holds the key

From that time Jesus began to preach and say, "Repent, for the kingdom of heaven is at hand.

—Matthew 4:17

There is no obesity in Heaven, so there should be no obesity on earth. Why has Satan been successful in his strategy to make you sick and overweight? Because of a lack of repentance in this area.

The will of God is done on earth as it is in Heaven as you align yourself with the Kingdom of God. Heaven must manifest in you to create a prosperous soul before you realize the will of God and his blessing at work in your life. You do that by changing the way you think.

Repent means to change your mind. The renewed mind repents continually so that the Word of God will dominate our thinking and lives.

> "Bad things happen to good people because good people make bad choices. They don't choose to make God's WORD final authority in their lives."[17]

Wherever you are experiencing failure, you know your mind is not renewed in that area because **God's Word NEVER fails!**

---

[17] Kenneth Copeland, "It's Time to get Healed," The Believer's Voice of Victory Broadcast Notes, October 25-29, 2021, p. 2

The power to lose weight is contained within the word *repent*. Change your mind to think as God thinks about your body, health, and weight. Change your mind, and you will change your life. Your thoughts always precede the direction of your life.

The prerequisite to repenting is discovering what God has said in His Word about your battle.

Double-minded

> Consider it wholly joyful, my brethren, whenever you are enveloped in or encounter trials of any sort or fall into various temptations. Be assured and understand that the trial and proving of your faith bring out endurance and steadfastness and patience. But let endurance and steadfastness and patience have full play and do a thorough work, so that you may be [people] perfectly and fully developed [with no defects], lacking in nothing. If any of you is deficient in wisdom, let him ask of the giving God [Who gives] to everyone liberally and ungrudgingly, without reproaching or faultfinding, and it will be given him. Only it must be in faith that he asks with no wavering (no hesitating, no doubting). For the one who wavers (hesitates, doubts) is like the billowing surge out at sea that is blown hither and thither and tossed by the wind. For truly, let not such a person imagine that he will receive anything [he asks for] from the Lord, [For being as he is] a man of two minds (hesitating, dubious, irresolute), [he is] unstable and unreliable and uncertain about everything [he thinks, feels, decides].
>
> –James 1:2-8 (AMPC)

"Double-mindedness is fluctuating between God's Word and people's opinions. It may occur when you act on what you *think* the Word says, instead of searching the Scriptures for yourself and finding out what God has promised."

"To avoid double-mindedness, stand firm in what you know to be true from God's Word. Don't allow room in your thinking for alternatives. Walk by faith—not according to your own understanding or the circumstances that surround you. Once you find out exactly what God has promised in His Word, apply that truth to your life. By standing firm in your agreement with God's Word, you are allowing the Lord to work freely to administer *His* best in the situation (see James 3:10-13)." [18]

If you know how to control your thoughts and feelings, you can eliminate any habit, including food idols. The thoughts and feelings in your unconscious mind empower your habits.

Double-mindedness is a split focus or division (di-vision, divided vision). Whatever you focus on the most will control the direction of your life.

Tony Robbins describes his training to drive a racecar. His instructor taught him when he goes into a skid, don't look at the wall. Look at where you want to go.

While practicing on the racetrack, the instructor forced the car into a skid. Tony instinctively looked at the wall despite the instructor's

---

[18] Kenneth Copeland Ministries, "Question of the Day," September 18, 2022, https://www.kcm.org/read/question-of-the-day

teaching. The instructor grabbed Tony's head and turned it in the direction the car should be going.

The car did not hit the wall after Tony turned his head.

You don't want to look at the wall because you will drive the car into the wall when that is your focus. The same principle is involved with repentance or changing your thinking. You will always move in the direction that your mind is focused. If you focus on "I'm overweight," you will keep getting the same.

Where there is no vision, the people are unrestrained, But happy is one who keeps the Law.

—Proverbs 29:18

Practice thinking, seeing yourself as fit and thin and refusing to see yourself as overweight. Meditate on scripture for healing and appetite control. Your focus now will help lead you to your goal.

For as he thinks within himself, so he is. He says to you, "Eat and drink!" But his heart is not with you.

—Proverbs 23:7

If your identity is rooted in thinking of yourself as fat, that is what you will be or remain. If you see and think of yourself the way God sees you as blessed, healed, prosperous, and at your ideal weight, your transformed mind will transform your body into the divine image created by the Word of God.

A double mind is a mind divided against itself. It is a mind that tries to operate in fear and faith simultaneously. Neither a divided mind nor a divided kingdom can stand. God answers faith, not unbelieving prayers. You cannot receive Kingdom benefits while you remain double-minded. Become Word-minded, and you will master your weight.

> And knowing their thoughts, Jesus said to them, "Every kingdom divided against itself is laid waste; and no city or house divided against itself will stand. And if Satan is casting out Satan, he has become divided against himself; how then will his kingdom stand?
>
> –Matthew 12:25-26

The double mind teeters between faith and unbelief

The double mind is unstable in all its ways. A double-minded person teeters-totters back and forth between believing and doubting. The single-minded person is decisive, fixed, firmly established, and not easily moved, shaken, or overthrown.

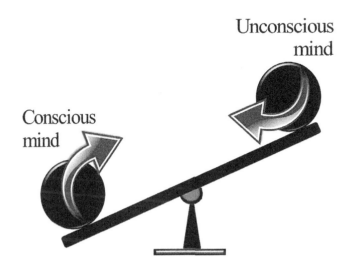

Make a quality decision to put the Word of God as the final authority in your life. A quality decision is one you commit wholeheartedly to and refuse to turn.

Refuse to be moved by what you see in the mirror. Stop weighing yourself until you renew your mind and are single-minded regarding what God's Word says about your health. When you look in the mirror, do not say curse words about yourself like "you fat thing" or "I'm getting heavier."

Instead, say, "I'm not moved by what I see, and I'm not moved by what I feel. I am moved only by the Word of God, and the Word says Christ has healed me. I receive my healing. My weight is at its optimal level (say your goal weight, such as 125 lbs. or 175 lbs.)."

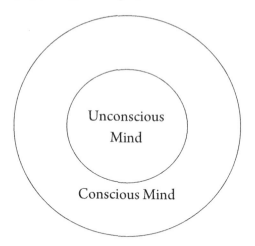

Conscious Mind Language
Logic & reasoning
Judges
Short-term memory
Determines good or bad
Thinks

Unconscious Mind Language
Emotions & imagination
Controls habits
Long-term memory
Protective
Reacts

For the desire of the flesh is against the Spirit, and the Spirit
against the flesh; for these are in opposition to one another,
to keep you from doing whatever you want.

–Galatians 5:17

Why willpower will not help you permanently lose weight

The will, located in the conscious mind, is like a bank account where you deposit credits or spend debits. However, the habit of craving food is in your unconscious mind.

Food cravings create a conflict between our conscious and unconscious minds. They are in a tug of war with each other. The conscious mind wants to control cravings and lose weight, while emotions or imaginations create food cravings in the unconscious mind.

As much as you try to use your will to manage your appetite, you still feel like a prisoner to these cravings. The problem is you're trying to use willpower to deliver yourself from the conscious mind while the cravings are in the unconscious mind.

You find that you can only temporarily control the cravings. You will deplete your will bank account very quickly since this is not an effective tool for change.

If I ask you to quit blinking your eyes, you can do that, right? However, you couldn't stop blinking your eyes for very long. Why? Because the control of eye blinking comes from the unconscious mind, not the conscious mind.

You can temporarily override the blinking with your conscious mind. However, the more you try to exert your willpower on this, the more your mind becomes obsessed with the idea of blinking your eyes.

The obsession is the nature of the mind war. The more you try to control cravings and habits with willpower, the more frustrated you become because your will cannot deliver you by itself. The solution is to renew your unconscious mind, uprooting the evil seed Satan planted in your heart by casting down imaginations until you become single-minded and firm in your decision without wavering. Do this, and you will be free of the cravings.

The single-mind model liberates a woman from a 30-year drug addiction

After 30 years of struggling with drug addiction and multiple failures with rehab, Marie became completely free in a two-hour session collaborating with me. She could walk free from a horrible habit in just one 2-hour session by resolving her double-mindedness. I helped her using the principles found in this book.

> "I would like to thank Bruce for helping me quit a drug addiction I have had for over 30 years. He truly worked a miracle. I had no idea quitting this lifelong addiction could be quick, easy, and painless. I am forever grateful to Bruce for helping me to turn my life around and be the person I have always wanted to be."

If the single-mind model can help someone break a 30-year drug habit, it can certainly help you break free of food cravings! The cure is to offer your body to the Lord as a living sacrifice and renew your mind resulting in God's will being perfected in your appetites and body. This is a grace-based approach to weight loss, rather than the striving-based system people are doomed to under the curse.

Therefore I urge you, brothers and sisters, by the mercies of God, to present your bodies as a living and holy sacrifice, acceptable to God, which is your spiritual service of worship. And do not be conformed to this world, but be transformed by the renewing of your mind, so that you may prove what the will of God is, that which is good and acceptable and perfect.

–Romans 12:1-2

Stop the struggle and rest while the Word of faith grows in your heart, transforming your mind and your body.

For the one who has entered His rest has himself also rested from his works, as God did from His. Therefore let's make every effort to enter that rest, so that no one will fall by following the same example of disobedience.

–Hebrews 4:10-11

I have never seen an orange tree struggle and groan to try to produce an orange. The tree rests in the soil and produces fruit without effort. In the same way, you can rest in the completed work of Jesus Christ, Who has redeemed you from the curse of the law, which includes sickness and excess weight.

When you decide to renew your mind, speak words of faith regarding your body and appetites, and live by EVERY word that proceeds from the mouth of God, the Word will transform your mind AND your body. Begin with *The Prayer of Repentance.*

The Prayer of Repentance

Dear Heavenly Father,

I repent of gluttony and food idols that were a substitute for faith in You. I ask that the Spirit of Truth will lead me into all truth regarding the foods I eat and teach me how to care appropriately for this temple, by avoiding dangerous foods and drinks that are toxic and produce inflammation. Lead me to eat healthy foods in quantities best for my health and weight.

Forgive me for being double-minded regarding my health, weight, and nutrition. I ask that you deliver me from craving sugar and all unhealthy foods. I declare by faith that I am now free from all cravings and food idols.

Thank You, Father. In Jesus' Name. Amen.

Action steps

1. Repent by making a quality decision to become single-minded and focused on God's Word, meditating on scriptures for healing and appetite control. You will find many of these scriptures in the chapter for Key 5 – *Prayer and Decrees.*

2. Immerse yourself in meditating and hearing the Word of God with specific scriptures that will help you lose weight and heal your body. Listen to anointed teachings on faith,

healing, Courts of Heaven, deliverance, and healing soul wounds throughout the day. Read books on these subjects.

KEY 3

PROSECUTE FOOD ADDICTIONS AND ALTAR IN THE COURTS OF HEAVEN

Prosecute Food Addictions and Altar in the Courts of Heaven

I kept looking
Until thrones were set up,
And the Ancient of Days took His seat;
His garment was white as snow,
And the hair of His head like pure wool.
His throne was ablaze with flames,
Its wheels were a burning fire.
[10] A river of fire was flowing
And coming out from before Him;
Thousands upon thousands were serving Him,
And myriads upon myriads were standing before Him;
The court convened,
And the books were opened.

—Daniel 7:9-10

"Any adversary in the spirit realm that is resisting God's Kingdom purpose for us will bow the knee to verdicts from the Court of Heaven. We have no need to yell, scream or even curse our foe. All we need is a legal precedent based on a verdict from Heaven and the fight is over. We then simply put into place the verdict that has been set down. This is where decrees come, but only after legality has been established." [19]

---

[19] Robert Henderson, "Operating in the Courts of Heaven," USA: Robert Henderson Ministries, 2014, (p. 21).

I will give you the keys of the kingdom of heaven; and whatever you bind on earth shall have been bound in heaven, and whatever you loose on earth shall have been loosed in heaven."

–Matthew 16:19

To succeed in spiritual warfare and receive answers to our prayers and decrees, they must align to God's will, just as the notches of a key must align to the tumblers within a lock to open a door.

Courts make legal decrees that either bind the guilty or loose the innocent. We bind what Heaven has bound and loose what Heaven has loosed.

And I saw heaven opened, and behold, a white horse, and He who sat on it is called Faithful and True, and in righteousness He judges and wages war. His eyes are a flame of fire, and on His head are many crowns; and He has a name written on Him which no one knows except Himself.

–Revelation 19:11

"We must learn to only make war based on judgements, decisions and verdicts that are received out of the courts of Heaven. To try to make war without a verdict and judgement from the court of Heaven is to suffer defeat and even satanic backlash because we have no legal footing to be there or be engaging in such activity. On the other hand, if we can get legal renderings concerning a situation in place, then we can march onto the battlefield and win every time. The problem has been that we have tried to win on the battlefield without legal verdicts from Heaven backing us up. We must learn how to get these verdicts and judgements in place so answers can come to our prayers and the Kingdom cause of Christ can land on the Earth."[20]

Kings have two primary responsibilities. The first is to command the military to protect and defend life and property. The second is to serve as a court judge to make legal decrees.

The Bible says that we are kings and priests. As priests, we access the throne of Heaven today and receive the revelation of God's will. With that revelation, we make legal decrees as kings with the authority that comes with the revelation into the earth to transform it into His will and Kingdom.

We are kings to adjudicate the Word of God from the Courts of Heaven.

Job's verdicts from the Courts of Heaven

Curses cannot attach to a person without a just, legal cause.

> *Like a sparrow in its flitting, like a swallow in its flying,*
> *So a curse without cause does not come to rest.*
>
> *–Proverbs 26:2*

Contrary to religious tradition, Job's sorrows were not random attacks. A specific legal cause gave Satan the right to attack Job. Satan did not attack Job because it was God's will for these disasters to happen to him.

---

[20] Robert Henderson, "Operating in the Courts of Heaven," USA: Robert Henderson Ministries, 2014, (p. 18).

Satan attacked Job because God did not have the legal right to protect him from those attacks. God could not protect Job without opposing His own Word, which would thereby divide His Kingdom.

Job violated the covenant with God because of his fear and unbelief. Fear and unbelief do not work in the Kingdom of God. Instead, they are weapons that Satan uses to get the legal right to attach a curse to a person.

> *Job's sons used to take turns giving a feast, to which all the others would come, and they always invited their three sisters to join them. The morning after each feast, Job would get up early and offer sacrifices for each of his children in order to purify them. He always did this because he thought that one of them might have sinned by insulting God unintentionally.*
>
> *–Job 1:4-5*

Job made continual sacrifices for his children because he doubted their character. He believed they were covenant breakers rather than covenant keepers. They had a lot of feasts because Job allowed them to spend his wealth without accountability. He was an overindulgent parent. The children's idol was Mammon, and Job's idol was his children. He placed them above God because he did not discipline them according to the covenant of God. He tolerated their behavior rather than confronting them about their sin.

Satan prosecutes Job before the Courts of Heaven

> *Now there was a day when the sons of God came to present themselves before the Lord, and Satan also came among them. The Lord said to Satan, "From where do you come?"*

Satan answered the Lord and said, "From roaming about on the earth and walking around on it." The Lord said to Satan, "Have you considered My servant Job? For there is no one like him on the earth, a blameless and upright man, fearing God and turning away from evil." Then Satan answered the Lord, "Does Job fear God for nothing? Have You not made a fence around him and his house and all that he has, on every side? You have blessed the work of his hands, and his possessions have increased in the land. But reach out with Your hand now and touch all that he has; he will certainly curse You to Your face." Then the Lord said to Satan, "Behold, all that he has is in your power; only do not reach out and put your hand on him." So Satan departed from the presence of the Lord.

–Job 1:6-12

Job had opened a door that gave Satan legal access to bring curses upon his life before the Courts of Heaven. Job broke the covenant fence of protection and provision God placed around him that previously restrained Satan from attacking his life.

Fear of anything other than God is a sin. Fear moves the devil, just like faith moves God. Fear gave the devil access to bring a curse and destroy Job.

For what I fear comes upon me,
And what I dread encounters me.

–Job 3:25

An idol does not have to have a physical form to be an idol. Before a man's hands could create an idol, it had to be created by his imagination. Therefore thoughts, cravings, and humanistic philosophies can be idols.

> *Since we are God's children, we should not suppose that his nature is anything like an image of gold or silver or stone, shaped by human art and skill.*
>
> *–Acts 17:29*

"**Idol**. Anything on which we set our affections; that to which we indulge an excessive and sinful attachment. 1 John 5:1 *Little children, keep yourselves from idols.*"

"An *idol* is anything which usurps the place of God in the hearts of his rational creatures." [21]

Peter, like Job, was tried in the Court of Heaven.

> *Simon, Simon, behold, Satan has demanded to sift you men like wheat; but I have prayed for you, that your faith will not fail; and you, when you have turned back, strengthen your brothers.*
>
> *–Luke 22:31-32*

The battle is in mind and emotions

You will struggle to lose weight if you do not realize that your battle is not with your body (flesh and blood), but with demonic spirits establishing strongholds within your mind. Strongholds are fortresses of demonic territory within our hearts that demons access

---

[21] Noah Webster, "American Dictionary of the English Language," Webster's Dictionary 1828, webstersdictionary1828.com/Dictionary/idol

legally through our sins and soul wounds. They guard their treasures with reasonings and accusations.

A stronghold is what demons erect within your heart so you will actively defend them against God's Word and the work of the Holy Spirit

Gluttony and food idols are demonic strongholds.

Suppose you justify the reason you can eat nutritional trash or unhealthy foods, or make jokes about your weight and fail to oppose the dysfunction and disease in your body. You thereby defend Satan's legal right to rule in your life. That is submission to Satan and resistance to God. That is idolatry and a stronghold.

Strongholds are foundations of Satan's work within a person's heart, whereby he exalts himself above the knowledge of God's Word. Seek the Lord, asking Him to reveal the demonic strategies they use to prevent you from reaching your weight goal. Then, release your faith for wisdom to overcome and destroy the strongholds.

> *Finally, be strong in the Lord and in the strength of His might. Put on the full armor of God, so that you will be able to stand firm against the schemes of the devil. For our struggle is not against flesh and blood, but against the rulers, against the powers, against the world forces of this darkness, against the spiritual forces of wickedness in the heavenly places.*
>
> *–Ephesians 6:10-12*

This word for wrestle is a variation of the word used in Revelation 12, meaning to *throw the accuser to the ground*. It speaks here of legal maneuverings to bind the devil.

> *Then I heard a loud voice in heaven, saying, "Now the salvation, and the power, and the kingdom of our God and the authority of His Christ have come, for the accuser of our brothers and sisters has been thrown down, the one who accuses them before our God day and night.*

–Revelation 12:10

The "accuser" in the original Greek language is *"kategoreo"* which means to accuse in a court of law.

Wrestle Satan to the ground and then hold him down with your foot on his head using your authority by faith. Cast Satan down under your feet anytime he accuses you of being overweight, unattractive, too weak, too undisciplined, a failure, or any other word-curse he hurls at you.

Refuse to agree with what Satan and the world say about you. Declare what God has said in His Word with your faith.

He said that you are:

- the righteousness of God in Christ Jesus;
- you are wise;
- you're a world overcomer;
- you're more than a conqueror;
- you're the head and not the tail;
- you are above only and not beneath;
- you're blessed coming in and going out;
- you have a prosperous soul;
- you are the healed;

- you are prosperous;
- you are filled full of joy.

The battle is also in the court

Genetics did not predestine your weight, but it is a result of you and your bloodline giving Satan legal access to afflict your body with sickness or poor health.

Sean was genetically disposed to weight problems when considering his bloodlines, but dealing with food cravings and following an easy exercise program resulted in significant weight loss.

"I lost over 40 pounds in four months!!! With this program, I could lose weight quickly, regain energy, and feel more comfortable in my skin. Bruce helped me to control my food cravings and produce a plan for success. I did not need a personal trainer or an expensive gym membership. I only exercised for 30 minutes per week. I could easily follow this program at the small gym in my neighborhood. I highly recommend this program to anyone who needs an easy program to follow to lose weight." —Sean T.

"I began to see that the reason people were not healed and died prematurely was because the devil had a legal right to hold them in sickness. If they were to be healed, this legal right had to be revoked in the Courts of Heaven."[22]

---

[22] Robert Henderson "Receiving Healing from the Courts of Heaven (The Official Courts of Heaven)," USA: Destiny Publishers, Inc., 2018, (p. 8).

Excess weight is a sickness, and God's divine will for you is to receive healing and your weight at an optimal level. If you have struggled to lose weight, Satan likely has a legal right to bind you with sickness.

The idols in your life and bloodline may be contributing to your excess weight. This discovery will help you prosecute the idols and their evil altars in the Court of Heaven to receive freedom and healing. A healthy body will move toward optimal weight as the Lord first restores your soul and then your body.

> He restores my soul; He guides me in the path of righteousness for His name's sake.
>
> –Psalm 23:3

> The Lord will sustain him upon his sickbed; In his illness, You restore him to health. As for me, I said, "Lord, be gracious to me; Heal my soul, for I have sinned against You.
>
> –Psalm 41:3-4

Evil idols and altars demand sacrifice. They never deliver what they promise in terms of comfort and satisfaction, which is why the evil altar craves and demands more sacrifice. What kind of sacrifice does an evil altar of gluttony and food addictions demand? Food.

Food idolatry is seeking other gods

> "While the Hebrew אֶחָד can mean "one," echad can also mean "alone." Here's a stronger translation of Deut 6:4: "Hear, O Israel, the Lord is our God, the Lord alone." That is, the Lord is Israel's God, and the people of Israel must "not go after other gods" (Deut 6:14); they must "love," or be "loyal" to, the Lord alone."

"You can break food addiction with the help of the Holy Spirit. Lay poor food choices on the altar. Ask God for supernatural help to walk away from them and overcome addiction. Use the fruit of the spirit—self-control—and say no. If you are getting ready to attend a social function, visualize yourself ahead of time saying 'No, thank you,' when offered something unhealthy." [23]

Do not allow love for food to overshadow your love for God.

Do not love the world nor the things in the world. If anyone loves the world, the love of the Father is not in him. For all that is in the world, the lust of the flesh and the lust of the eyes and the boastful pride of life, is not from the Father, but is from the world. The world is passing away and also its lusts; but the one who does the will of God continues to live forever.

–1 John 2:15-17

"I love how much of the glory of God in creation is edible. It is a sweet thing that God created a pleasurable world of food. But that pleasure of food is meant to be a finger that points me to God. It is not meant to be the thing that satisfies my heart." [24]

By breaking curses, destroying evil altars, and ending Satan's legal right to attack your soul and body, you can put an end to gluttony and food idols.

---

[23] Don Colbert, MD, "How to Lose Weight God's Way," Kenneth Copeland Ministries, https://www.kcm.org/real-help/life-work/learn/how-lose-weight-gods-way?language_content_entity=en-US

[24] Paul Tripp, "Interview with Paul Tripp," Desiring God, February 2, 2016, https://www.desiringgod.org/interviews/the-spiritual-battle-with-weight-loss

Their end is destruction, their god is their belly, and they glory in their shame, with minds set on earthly things.

–Philippians 3:19

Be not among drunkards or among gluttonous eaters of meat, for the drunkard and the glutton will come to poverty, and slumber will clothe them with rags.

–Proverbs 23:20-21

You have the legal right to bind any attack against you, even excess weight, in the Court of Heaven.

To learn more about the Courts of Heaven, evil altars, and idols, read:

Operating in the Courts of Heaven by Robert Henderson

Dangerous Prayers from the Courts of Heaven that Destroy Evil Altars by Dr. Francis Myles

Idols Riot by Katie Souza and Dr. Francis Myles

Action steps

1. Schedule one hour to pray and seek the Lord to reveal demonic strategies and strongholds regarding your weight.

2. Listen to the Holy Spirit and make a list of these.

3. Ask the Lord to give you specific scriptures to build your faith to conquer the strongholds by meditating and decreeing these over your life (you can find several in Key 5).

KEY 4

FILE A LAWSUIT IN THE COURTS OF HEAVEN TO LOSE WEIGHT

Courts of Heaven prayer against gluttony and the idol of food addiction

Worship

Worship as the Holy Spirit leads you.

Request the court to be seated

Heavenly Father, I ask for the Court of Heaven to be seated according to Daniel 7:9-10.

Oh, Righteous Judge and Sovereign Ruler of Heaven and earth, please open the books of destiny as I stand before the Court of Heaven to plead my case so I can be justified.

I ask You, Heavenly Father, to permit me to stand before this Court of Heaven today according to my legal rights as a citizen of the Kingdom of God. I ask this according to the rights secured for me through the blood of the covenant of Jesus Christ. He has granted the righteousness of Christ to me by faith with all its rights and privileges.

I am here today to seek the Court's righteous judgement against the idol and altar of gluttony and food addictions that the devil, the accuser, and adversary, has inserted into my bloodline.

Oh, Righteous Judge, I call Heaven and earth to be witnesses of record today regarding this holy litigation against the evil altar of gluttony and food addictions.

I decree that this evil altar of gluttony and food addiction will not kill, injure, cause excess weight gain, or cause sickness of the bodies or souls of my family, future generations, or myself.

Surrender rights to represent self to the Lord Jesus Christ

Heavenly Father, I stand in the presence of this court with my Heavenly legal representative, the Holy Spirit, my eternal counselor. I call upon my defense attorney and advocate, according to my legal right for representation according to the New Covenant, the Lord Jesus Christ, to defend my interests before this High Court and plead my case against the evil altar of gluttony and food addiction that the devil inserted into my ancestral line. I surrender all rights to self-advocacy.

I ask that the Holy Spirit lead me into all truth and reality as a son of God to make me fully informed of the proceedings of this court so I may successfully litigate the evil altar of gluttony and food addiction in this court in the name of Jesus.

Subpoena the evil altar and idol of gluttony and food addiction

Righteous Judge, I subpoena the altar of gluttony and food addiction in my bloodline and the idol that attends it to appear before this divine courtroom to answer the charges that I bring and prosecute a covenantal lawsuit against them in the name of Jesus.

Oh, Righteous Judge, I judge these demonic spirits by the authority this court has invested in me through the New Covenant of Jesus Christ.

I will present my case through my advocate, Jesus Christ, and stand in judgement against these demonic spirits. I do this according to that authority given to me in the name of Jesus Christ because the Word of God declares:

Do you not know that we will judge angels? How much more matters of this life?

- 1 Corinthians 6:3

Address the devil's accusations

Heavenly Father, I enter the guilty plea into the court's records. It is written:

Come to good terms with your accuser quickly, while you are with him on the way to court, so that your accuser will not hand you over to the judge, and the judge to the officer, and you will not be thrown into prison.

–Matthew 5:25

Heavenly Father, I am aware that my adversary, the devil, accuses me before this court even as he does all men on the earth. During these proceedings, I intend to cast him down and break any legal ties he may have found to accuse me, according to my authority, in the name of Jesus Christ.

The Word of God declares:

Then I heard a loud voice in heaven, saying, "Now the salvation, and the power, and the kingdom of our God and the authority of His Christ have come, for the accuser of our brothers and sisters has been thrown down, the one who accuses them before our God day and night. And they overcame him because of the blood of the Lamb and because of the word of their testimony, and they did not love their life even when faced with death.

–Revelation 12:10-11

These signs will accompany those who have believed: in My name they will cast out demons, they will speak with new tongues;

–Mark 16:17

Now He called the twelve together and gave them power and authority over all the demons, and the power to heal diseases.

–Luke 9:1

I agree with the accusations brought by the devil against my bloodline and me. I confess that those accusations are true if this court deems them legitimate. I plead guilty to all charges related to idolatry. I submit my guilty plea to the court in Jesus' Name.

I humbly repent and ask You to forgive me of all the charges filed against me, personal and generational sins, and soulish wounds connected to evil altars, gluttony, and food idols. I repent for pursuing idols to obtain comfort when my soul was fractured.

I repent for seeking idols to attempt to fulfill my needs instead of standing steadfast on the Word of God by faith to see the fulfillment of my promises.

I repent of stuffing my emotions with food instead of confessing the Lordship of Jesus Christ over my area of need for healing and comfort.

I repent of having other gods and idols before You, such as my appetites. The Word of God declares:

whose end is destruction, whose god is their appetite, and whose glory is in their shame, who have their minds on earthly things.

–Philippians 3:19

I repent for allowing myself to be a slave to my appetites. I now exchange my shame for Your righteousness for cleansing and forgiveness. I ask that all these sins be cleansed from my bloodline also.

I repent of holding any offense or unforgiveness toward anyone. Please forgive me for all of my unforgiveness. You can now answer my prayers, for the Word of God declares:

And whenever you stand praying, forgive, if you have anything against anyone so that your Father who is in heaven will also forgive you for your offenses. But if you do not forgive, neither will your Father who is in heaven forgive your offenses.

–Mark 11:24-25

I repent for everything I have in common with idols and evil altars. I repent for anything in my heart that is blocking the healing of my body and losing weight.

I repent for all generational soul wounds, word curses, all idle, inoperative, useless words of doubt and unbelief spoken by myself and my bloodline.

I renounce all covenants made by myself or my bloodline with all demonic spirits, evil altars, and idols.

I thank You, Heavenly Father, that the decrees of this court agree with me that all these demonic covenants with evil altars are held null and void, rendered harmless and useless against my bloodline and me.

Let the court remove all word curses from the court records because forgiveness is granted to my bloodline and me by Jesus Christ.

Let the court record show that I have now given back to the devil everything he claims against my bloodline and me. The blood of Jesus cancels all legal claims against my bloodline and me! I declare a divorce against the devil.

Petition the blood of Jesus to forgive and cleanse from all unrighteousness

I petition the court to acknowledge that according to the covenant I have in the blood of Jesus Christ, I am now forgiven and cleansed of all unrighteousness. Christ redeemed me from all curses.

I have repented and confessed my sins. Therefore, Satan has no legal right to accuse me before the court.

I declare that because of Christ, I stand justified and made righteous before the court, as though I have never sinned in my life.

It is written:

He made Him who knew no sin to be sin in our behalf, so that we might become the righteousness of God in Him.

–2 Corinthians 5:21

For if by the offense of the one, death reigned through the one, much more will those who receive the abundance of grace and of the gift of righteousness reign in life through the One, Jesus Christ.

–Romans 5:17

I petition the court to acknowledge that I am a new creation in Christ Jesus. I remove the old things of evil altars, idols, sins, sickness, excess weight, and all curses by faith. They no longer have any legal right to attach themselves to me.

The Word of God declares:

If we confess our sins, He is faithful and righteous, so that He will forgive us our sins and cleanse us from all unrighteousness.

–1 John 1:9

Therefore if anyone is in Christ, this person is a new creation; the old things passed away; behold, new things have come.

–2 Corinthians 5:17

Righteous Judge, I decree that by the covenant blood of Jesus and His grace, the court will acquit me of all charges brought against my bloodline and me for all these sins and all curses reversed in Jesus' Name.

Therefore, I request that this court now dismiss all charges and accusations brought against my bloodline and me in Jesus' name.

I cast down the accuser, my adversary, the devil, with all his accusations against my bloodline and me, in Jesus' name.

Request the court to dispatch angels to enforce the judgement against the evil Altar and idol

Oh, Righteous Judge, I ask that You dispatch angels to enforce the judgement of this court against the evil altar and idol of gluttony and food addictions planted in my bloodline and deliver me in Jesus's name.

According to my legal rights in the covenant, I decree the destruction of this evil altar. The Word of God declares:

Are they not all ministering spirits, sent out to provide service for the sake of those who will inherit salvation?

–Hebrews 1:14

The angel of the Lord encamps around those who fear Him, And rescues them.

–Psalm 34:7

Present scriptural evidence for a divine restraining order

Heavenly Father, I present the following scriptural evidence against the spirit and evil altar of gluttony and food addictions in my life and bloodline:

Do not be with heavy drinkers of wine,
Or with gluttonous eaters of meat;
For the heavy drinker and the glutton will come to poverty,
And drowsiness will clothe one with rags.

–Proverbs 23:20-21

But the fruit of the Spirit is love, joy, peace, patience, kind-
ness, goodness, faithfulness, gentleness, self-control; against
such things there is no law.

–Galatians 5:22-23

We know that no one who has been born of God sins; but He
who was born of God keeps him, and the evil one does not
touch him.

–1 John 5:18

Heavenly Father, based on this scriptural evidence, the court can see that if the court does not restrain the spirit and the evil altar of gluttony and food addiction, they would cause significant damage and hinder the purposes of God as to my own life and destiny.

I request that the court revoke every legal right of the evil altar and their attending spirit over my life now in the name of Jesus. I also ask for a divine restraining order against the spirit and altar of gluttony and food addictions in Jesus' name.

Decrees of healing and sealing the just verdict and court records

Oh, Righteous Judge, based on what Christ has provided for me in the New Covenant, I revoke by legal decree all resistance of the devil against my ability to lose weight and walk in divine health. Jesus paid off the debt for my transgressions and canceled the legal charges against me. Satan no longer has legal bounds to harass or vex me concerning my health and weight.

The Word of God declares:

having canceled the certificate of debt consisting of decrees against us, which was hostile to us; and He has taken it out of the way, having nailed it to the cross.

–Colossians 2:14

The Spirit of the Lord God is upon me, Because the Lord anointed me To bring good news to the humble; He has sent me to bind up the brokenhearted, To proclaim release to captives And freedom to prisoners;

–Isaiah 61:1

Based upon this scriptural evidence, I now decree before this court that I possess what Jesus has given to me as gifts, divine healing, and weight loss. He bore my sins in His own body, and with the wounds upon His body, I am healed and delivered of excess weight.

Jesus has healed me In every area of my body and soul.

I am healed and delivered of every soul wound Satan used to attack me.

I now declare that all my glands and hormones are healed and in perfect balance.

Jesus has healed me of any accompanying diseases to being overweight.

Jesus has healed me of every sickness and disease in the name of Jesus!

Oh, Righteous Judge, I ask that You adjourn the proceedings in the name of Jesus Christ, Amen!

Communion

Now receive communion. Declare your redemption from the curse of the law according to Galatians 3:13-14, and decree all the blessings of Deuteronomy 28:1-14.

KEY 5

PRAY & MAKE FAITH DECREES

Enforce the Court of Heaven's verdict

Now that you have a verdict against your adversary, the devil, from the Court of Heaven, what's next? As you may know from the natural world, a court decree is useless unless someone enforces the law. That someone is you.

Your responsibility is to decree your faith based upon the legal decrees of the Word of God and the Courts of Heaven. No place in the Bible did Jesus ever cast out a devil merely by thinking him out.

He spoke faith-filled words by the power of the Holy Spirit that drove demons out of people. You bind the enemy's attempt to make you sick and overweight by speaking what the Word of God says about healing and appetites.

> *The godly ones shall be jubilant in glory;*
> *They shall sing for joy on their beds.*
> *The high praises of God shall be in their mouths,*
> *And a two-edged sword in their hands,*
> *To execute vengeance on the nations,*
> *And punishment on the peoples,*
>
> *To bind their kings with chains,*
> *And their dignitaries with shackles of iron,*
> *To execute against them the judgement written.*
> *This is an honor for all His godly ones.*
> *Praise the Lord!*
>
> *–Psalm 149:5-9*

Now when the unclean spirit comes out of a person, it passes through waterless places seeking rest, and does not find it. Then it says, 'I will return to my house from which I came'; and when it comes, it finds it unoccupied, swept, and put in order. Then it goes and brings along with it seven other spirits more wicked than itself, and they come in and live there; and the last condition of that person becomes worse than the first. That is the way it will also be with this evil generation.

–Matthew 12:43-45

Your faith decrees are the supernatural weapons God has given you to execute the righteous verdicts in the Word of God and issued from the Courts of Heaven. With the two-edged sword in your mouth, you bind Satan's attacks against your body that cause the weight gain so that he is rendered harmless and ineffective against you. When he is bound, you lose weight and increase in divine health.

And take the helmet of salvation and the sword of the Spirit, which is the word of God.

–Ephesians 6:17

For the word of God is living and active, and sharper than any two-edged sword, even penetrating as far as the division of soul and spirit, of both joints and marrow, and able to judge the thoughts and intentions of the heart.

–Hebrews 4:12

You don't have a weight problem. You have a word problem. You speak words that will condemn you to be sick and fat, or justify you to be thin and healed. You must choose.

I call heaven and earth to witness against you today that I have placed before you life and death, the blessing and the curse. So choose life in order that you may live, you and your descendants,

–Deuteronomy 30:19

When you change your words and thoughts, you will change your body.

This Book of the Law shall not depart from your mouth, but you shall meditate on it day and night, so that you may be careful to do according to all that is written in it; for then you will make your way prosperous, and then you will achieve success.

–Joshua 1:8

God told Joshua three things you must do to be successful.

1. Speak God's Word. When Moses sent the 12 spies to investigate the promised land, two came back, speaking a good report (Joshua and Caleb), and the other 10 declared an evil account of doubt and unbelief. On their return to the camp, the Israelites believed and repeated the bad report. God judged them because of their words of unbelief. They wandered in the wilderness for 40 years. Speak words of faith concerning your weight and refuse words of doubt. Do not speak what the scale or tape measure says. Speak your desired result for weight loss instead.

2. Meditate on God's Word. Let the Word of God dominate your thinking and remove the mountains of food addictions, hormonal imbalance, and excess weight.

3. Now act on the Word. Faith is an act. You should already have direction on eating healthy, exercising, and balancing your hormones.

But I tell you that for every careless word that people speak, they will give an account of it on the day of judgement. For by your words you will be justified, and by your words you will be condemned.

—Matthew 12:36-37

Truly I say to you, whoever says to this mountain, 'Be taken up and thrown into the sea,' and does not doubt in his heart, but believes that what he says is going to happen, it will be granted to him.

—Mark 11:23

If you can control the words you speak, then your words of faith will regulate your body, aligning with God's Word and will. Before you discipline your body, first discipline the words you speak. Speak words of faith declaring that you are, by faith, at your ideal weight, whatever the number is. Speak words of faith about your appetites. Speak words of faith and declare your hormones and the microbiome in your gut are in balance. Your words of faith will transform first your mind and then your body.

Control of your body, including your appetites, metabolism, hormones, every system, and every cell of your body, is related to the words you speak. Control your words, and you will manage your weight.

For we all stumble in many ways. If anyone does not stumble in what he says, he is a perfect man, able to rein in the whole body as well.

—James 3:2

Continue to speak faith-filled words over your weight and body throughout the day and every day until you can see the manifestation of your faith, just as the woman with the issue of blood received healing through her faith.

> *A woman who had had a hemorrhage for twelve years, and had endured much at the hands of many physicians, and had spent all that she had and was not helped at all, but instead had become worse— after hearing about Jesus, she came up in the crowd behind Him and touched His cloak. For she had been saying to herself, "If I just touch His garments, I will get well." And immediately the flow of her blood was dried up; and she felt in her body that she was healed of her disease. And immediately Jesus, perceiving in Himself that power from Him had gone out, turned around in the crowd and said, "Who touched My garments?" And His disciples said to Him, "You see the crowd pressing in on You, and You say, 'Who touched Me?'" And He looked around to see the woman who had done this. But the woman, fearing and trembling, aware of what had happened to her, came and fell down before Him and told Him the whole truth. And He said to her, "Daughter, your faith has made you well; go in peace and be cured of your disease.*
>
> –Mark 5:25-34
>
> *For she had been saying to herself, "If I just touch His garments, I will get well."*
>
> –Mark 5:28

Notice that the woman didn't say just one time that she would get well. She continued to say, *"If I just touch His garments, I will get well."*

Continue to speak the decrees and prayers in this book. Memorize one or two that you can say throughout the day. You will thereby meditate on it every time you say it. Keep declaring your weight goal as if you have already reached it. Do not say, "I will be at this weight by (some date)." Instead, say, "I have my faith weight goal now."

Jesus said it was her faith that made her well. Your faith will make you healthy and thin.

Prayer before meals and snacks

Recall what you have previously learned about focus and renewing the mind. I encourage you to write out or print this prayer and carry it with you wherever you go to maintain your focus and faith.

Pray it before every meal and snack. Your faith will be activated as your mind becomes focused on your faith goal to eat and live a healthy lifestyle. You thereby defeat Satan's temptations to destroy you with food addictions.

You will become more mindful of what you eat and eliminate the constant cravings and eating.

Heavenly Father,

I thank You for Your provision and blessings as You give me my daily bread. I ask that You not lead me into temptation but deliver me from evil food addictions and the sin of gluttony. Create in me a desire to eat healthy foods in quantities that are best for me, with the help of the Holy Spirit. My passion is to glorify You in my spirit, soul, and body.

I decree and declare that t he life and healing of Jesus manifests in my body. I give my body to You as a living sacrifice. I will not fall into

Satan's temptations to eat from the tree of the knowledge of good and evil, but I eat from the tree of life.

I live in contentment and satisfaction which I know that only You can provide. I can do anything, and everything, including lose weight, through Christ Who strengthens me and infuses me with inner power.

I'm free from all idols because Jesus Christ is my Lord! I declare that the Son has set me free. I am free from being overweight and sick. I am free of food idols. I declare that I refuse to wear the yoke of slavery to food idols, sickness, or excess weight because I am f ree in Christ. I refuse to serve any other master!

Thank You for Your abundant provision for me and that I will never lack any good thing because of Your magnificent promises.

I call this food blessed and sanctified in Jesus' name!

Weight loss prayer

Lord Jesus, You sacrificed Your body for me. Now I dedicate my body and appetite to You, surrendering my members and faculties as a living sacrifice, holy and acceptable to You as my reasonable act of worship. I eat to live rather than live to eat.

The world will not conform me to its way of eating and living, but the Word of God transforms me as I renew my mind to prove God's good, acceptable, and perfect will. I covenant with You now that I will maintain complete control of my appetite, restrain from food lusts, and speak words of faith, life, and healing over my body by the power of the Holy Spirit and the power of Your Word.

I declare by faith that Christ has set me free from slavery to food idols, slow metabolism, and hormonal imbalance because Jesus healed me from these dysfunctions and delivered me from the soul wounds that have driven my self-destructive relationship with food. I refuse to sacrifice my soul and body to satisfy food idols.

I received my deliverance and my healthy new body by faith, and thank You for it, Lord, in the name of Jesus Christ. Amen!

Scriptures for prayers

The following scriptures were the basis for the prayers above. They are given here so you have the option to copy and paste them into a journal, write or print them out, or save on your computer desktop or device to keep them handy to read, confess, memorize and meditate on through out the day.

Give us this day our daily bread.

–Matthew 6:11

And do not lead us into temptation, but deliver us from evil.

–Matthew 6:13

Do you not know that you are a temple of God and that the Spirit of God dwells in you?

–1 Corinthians 3:16

Therefore I urge you, brothers and sisters, by the mercies of God, to present your bodies as a living and holy sacrifice, acceptable to God, which is your spiritual service of worship. And do not be conformed to this world, but be transformed by the renewing of your mind, so that you may prove what the will of God is, that which is good and acceptable and perfect.

–Romans 12:1-2

The Lord God commanded the man, saying, "From any tree of the garden you may freely eat; but from the tree of the knowledge of good and evil you shall not eat, for on the day that you eat from it you will certainly die.

–Genesis 2:16-17

But if the Spirit of Him who raised Jesus from the dead dwells in you, He who raised Christ Jesus from the dead will also give life to your mortal bodies through His Spirit who dwells in you.

–Romans 8: 11

Not that I speak from need, for I have learned to be content in whatever circumstances I am. I know how to get along with little, and I also know how to live in prosperity; in any and every circumstance I have learned the secret of being filled and going hungry, both of having abundance and suffering need. I can do all things through Him who strengthens me.

–Philippians 4: 11

Beloved, I urge you as foreigners and strangers to abstain from fleshly lusts, which wage war against the soul.

–1 Peter 2:11

that you abstain from things sacrificed to idols, from blood, from things strangled, and from acts of sexual immorality; if you keep yourselves free from such things, you will do well. Farewell.

–Acts 15:29

> *So if the Son sets you free, you really will be free.*
>
> *–John 8:36*
>
> *It was for freedom that Christ set us free; therefore keep standing firm and do not be subject again to a yoke of slavery.*
>
> *–Galatians 5:1*

How to lose weight God's way

Don't say:

- "I have bad genes—my whole family is overweight."
- "Every time I lose weight, I just put it right back on."
- "I just love junk food."
- "No matter how hard I try, I just can't lose weight."
- "This is just who I am."

Do say:

- "I break every generational curse coming against my weight loss right now in the Name of Jesus!"
- "I am going to lose this weight for the glory of God!"
- "Thank You, God, that I am losing weight. Thank You that I've lost 5 pounds."
- "I take authority over food addiction right now in Jesus' Name!"[25]

---

[25] Dr. Don Colbert, "How to Lose Weight God's Way," Kenneth Copeland Ministries, https://secure.kcm.org.au/realhelp/how-lose-weight-gods-way/

Faith decrees for your breakthrough

Here are additional faith decrees you can speak to create greater health, control over your appetites and weight. God created the world with faith-filled words and you can create greater health and weight control following His example.

- I decree that my body is becoming healthier and stronger every day.
- I confess that I now desire only healthy foods; unhealthy foods will never control me again in the name of Jesus.
- Food fuels me rather than entertains me.
- I am in perfect peace because I keep my mind on the Lord. Therefore, I make sure that I am in a state of calm before I eat.
- I will never confess frustration again because I have perfect peace in Christ.

  The steadfast of mind You will keep in perfect peace,
  Because he trusts in You.

  –Isaiah 26:3

- I'm born of God. I have overcome the world with my faith; therefore, I have conquered weight gain. I am at my perfect weight.

  You are from God, little children, and have overcome them; because greater is He who is in you than he who is in the world.

  –1 John 4:4

- I am always in control of what I eat in Jesus' name.

  For God has not given us a spirit of timidity, but of power and love and discipline.

  –2 Timothy 1:7

- I discern and separate all emotions from hunger. I only eat when I am in a state of peace, and I am physically hungry and not because emotions are agitated.

  Do not be anxious about anything, but in everything by prayer and pleading with thanksgiving let your requests be made known to God. And the peace of God, which surpasses all comprehension, will guard your hearts and minds in Christ Jesus.

  –Philippians 4:6-7

- I love and respect my God-created body as the temple of the Lord, and I treat it healthily.

  Or do you not know that your body is a temple of the Holy Spirit within you, whom you have from God, and that you are not your own?

  –1 Corinthians 6:19

- My spirit and body belong to the Lord, and I honor Him in everything I do. I praise Him when I eat all my meals, keeping my body under control.

  but I strictly discipline my body and make it my slave, so that, after I have preached to others, I myself will not be disqualified.

  –1 Corinthians 9:27

- I eat to live and not live to eat.

  The good man eats to live, while the evil man lives to eat.

  –Proverbs 13:25 (TLB)

- I submit my body and appetite to God. I resist the devil, and I resist food cravings. They run from me now.

Submit therefore to God. But resist the devil, and he will flee from you.

−James 4:7

- Jesus was wounded so that He may heal me. He took away my weaknesses, food cravings, and soul wounds and bore away my diseases, physical dysfunctions, excess weight, hormonal imbalances, digestive dysfunctions, and slow metabolism. My new weight is (decree your weight goal).

    This happened so that what was spoken through Isaiah the prophet would be fulfilled: "He Himself took our illnesses and carried away our diseases."

    Matthew 8:17

- I declare by the authority of the Word of God that I am delivered from all soul wounds.

- I declare by the power of the Word of God that I have a restored and prosperous soul.

- I am strong and full of energy.

    Beloved, I pray that in all respects you may prosper and be in good health, just as your soul prospers.

    −3 John 2

CONCLUSION

In conclusion, we have learned five keys to present your case to Supernaturally Lose Weight in the Courts of Heaven:

Key 1: *Discern the Spiritual War on Your Weight* – This key will unlock revelation that will help you to discern the demonic spiritual war raging against your soul to wound you and rob your life and health;

Key 2: *Renew Your Mind* – Why willpower will not help you permanently lose weight and how to stop the warfare raging against your soul that causes you to gain weight;

Key 3: *Prosecute Food Addictions and Altars in the Courts of Heaven* – This key reveals how to break Satan's legal rights to keep you sick and overweight;

Key 4: *File a Lawsuit in the Courts of Heaven to Lose Weight* – This key reveals how to file a lawsuit against evil altars and idols and obtain a legal verdict in your favor for freedom from sickness and excess weight;

Key 5: *Pray & Make Faith Decrees* – This key reveals scriptures, prayers, and faith decrees to enforce the judicial verdict and allow you to lose weight without struggle.

Diets do not work. Instead, you need a lifestyle change. A Kingdom lifestyle is one in which you can do ALL things through Christ Who empowers you. A lifestyle is soul and body transformation created by reversing the curse, renewing the mind, and speaking faith-filled words over your health and weight.

You can accelerate your path to success through the process called immersion. You do this by putting your attention upon the Word of God. You spend more time reading, hearing, and meditating on the truths you hear until the word saturates your thinking and becomes a fortress around your heart and emotions.

> *My son, pay attention to my words;*
> *Incline your ear to my sayings.*
> *They are not to escape from your sight;*
> *Keep them in the midst of your heart.*
> *For they are life to those who find them,*
> *And healing to all their body.*
> *Watch over your heart with all diligence,*
> *For from it flow the springs of life.*
>
> *–Proverbs 4:20-23*

To help you renew your mind using the concept of immersion, I offer you a free audio download of this book. Please visit Gift.CourtsofHeavenWeightLoss.com for your download.

IN APPRECIATION

To Donna Partow for teaching and coaching me with her great insight and many years of experience on how to write a great book.

To Tamara Shaw, Christina Pearce, and Mickey Strickland for your feedback, editing suggestions, and encouragement. Karen Baily for help on graphics.

I HOPE YOU ENJOYED READING THIS BOOK

If you enjoyed this book, please give a big favor to future readers and help me. Please take a minute to write a review. It's easy to do!

Future readers and I will be very grateful.

Just visit the link below, which will take you directly to the correct page:

review.courtsofheavenweightloss.com.

Thank you very much for your review. It means a lot to me as an author and a coach. Plus, you are sowing Kingdom seed into the lives of others so that you also receive a harvest of righteousness and gifts from the Lord.

Thank you for reading my book.

ABOUT THE AUTHOR

Bruce Townsend is a gospel minister, marketplace minister, entrepreneur, and life coach. Bruce received his call from the Lord to be a prophet to the nations in 1978 and has moved in prophetic gifts over multiple decades.

Bruce has been a local church pastor, church planter alongside his ministry team, director of operations of a network of churches, and Christian school teacher. He has managed and owned multiple businesses.

As a therapist and life coach, Bruce has helped hundreds of people to stop smoking with a 97% scientifically proven success rate, and considerable numbers of people set free of alcohol and drug habits, as well as helping people to lose weight.

Bruce became a certified herbalist in 1996. He believes from a study of scripture that the streams of natural health and supernatural healing are flowing into one mighty river of revelation to restore God's people to divine health and long life to advance the Kingdom of God powerfully.

He believes that we are beginning to experience the most significant spiritual warfare ever at the same time, the beginning wave of the most extraordinary move of God on the earth. God's Kingdom mountain, Mt. Zion, is progressively filling the world. God is exalting His mountain above all the mountains and kingdoms of the earth (Daniel 2:34-35; Isaiah 2:1-4).

Bruce believes we're in a unique time to add the convergence of what he calls the 4R's, Revival, Restoration, Reformation, and Reconstruction. Salvation is coming not only to the greatest of people ever harvested for the Kingdom of God but also for cultures and nations, according to Matthew 28:18-20.

You can connect with Bruce at brucetownsend.com.

Made in United States
Orlando, FL
18 March 2023